Poised for Flight

poems by

Rosie Prohías Driscoll

Finishing Line Press
Georgetown, Kentucky

Poised for Flight

Publisher: Leah Huete de Maines
Editor: Christen Kincaid
Cover Art: Martin Arias
Author Photo: Susan Mulligan Fleischman
Cover Design: Elizabeth Maines McCleavy

Order online: www.finishinglinepress.com
            also available on amazon.com

Author inquiries and mail orders:
Finishing Line Press
P. O. Box 1626
Georgetown, Kentucky 40324
U. S. A.

Table of Contents

I. Prologue

Raíces..3

II. Ceiba Roots

Abacus...7
José Basilio...8
Sisa...9
Lutgardita...11
Clouds of Grief..12
Papá del Loro..13
Despedida I...14
Translating Aída..15
Wedding Bell..16
Rescue Operations...17
Feathers...18
Sueños...19
The Things She Carried...20
Excavation..22

III. Mangrove Roots

Labyrinths..25
Havana 1974...26
Ophelia Dying...28
Abuela Makes Natilla..29
Palabras for Coco..30
Diagramming Sentences..32
Poem In Which I Find My Mother....................................34
Love Language..35
Last Words...36

Despedida II 37

Triduum 39

¿Y Tu Abuela Dónde Está? 41

Love Letters, 1960-63 42

Shark Swimming 43

Cachita At My Throat 45

Relajo en el Carajo 47

Primo 48

Cross Currents 50

On Our Second Night in Havana 51

In the Absence of Paper 52

Lasciate Ogni Revisited 53

IV. The Canopy

Prayer for Grace 57

Inheritance 58

The Color of Music 59

First Flown 61

Broken Things 63

Dar a Luz 64

Breaking Open the Word 65

In Defense of Wheelbarrows 67

Etymologies 68

God Heals 69

Word Blossoms 70

When My First Daughter Tells Me 71

My Second Daughter Writes a Poem 72

Ring of Light 73

Colando Café 74

For Mami, my towering ceiba,
and for Ana and Sofia, my pajaritos in flight

Prologue

A la raíz va el hombre verdadero.
Radical no es más que eso: el que va a las raíces.
José Martí

Raíces

Madre
Hija de Oshún

      sprung from ceiba roots
      whose towering skirts enfold

the souls of Yoruban slaves
and Spanish guajiros seeking
protection from storm

Hija
Daughter of Elegguá

      fashioned by trickster hands
      mangrove child of twisted roots

replanted in salt currents
teeming with intertidal life
at the crossroads of land and sea

Roots shoot
skyward bloom

      massive limbs leafy
      tendrils entwined

weaving the lavish canopy
that will harbor
los pajaritos poised for flight

Ceiba Roots

Build altars in the places where I have reminded you who I am
and I will come and bless you there.
Exodus 20:24

Abacus

Cuéntame

Mami, tell me a story
count me

and see
how each of your memories
adds to the sum of me

José Basilio

You never spoke of your years in Tampa, where
los españoles exiled you and Manuel María

when they discovered you sold them the horses
you and your brothers raised at El Inglés

only to turn around and alert los mambises
to the date and time of the transaction,

stripping them of their horses, their money, and
their honor in a cloud of thundering hooves and dust.

We know only that on the day of departure, Sisa gave
you a box containing the viandas for an ajiaco cubano

—yuca, ñame, maíz, malanga, plátano, boniato—
and a note she wrote in her determined script:

Para que no te olvides de lo que dejaste en Cuba

Sisa

prepares the parlor, purposefully
placing the moisés that holds her
newborn César—el hijo de la vejez,
she calls him, born in her forty-second year—
under the piano so that he will not need quiet

to be quiet, but will grow accustomed
to the animated voices of the ladies
who come de visita, and her own voice
rising and falling among them,
retelling the stories of her youth.

Los cuenta like rosary beads. Como de niña
en Madruga her mother taught her to sew as Sisa
tucked herself into the folds of Lutgardita's skirt,
enabling them, viuda y huérfana, to earn enough
to buy una libra de arroz, un saco de frijoles.

Or how, as they cut yards of rayadillo to make
uniformes para los españoles, Lutgardita
se dio cuenta que el colonel would likely not
miss a few extra yards set aside surreptitiously
to clothe los mambises who came to her door

como—¿lo puedes creer?—José Martí did
one languid afternoon. Sisa's eyes grew wide
as he stepped softly into la sala, removed his
jipijapa and asked Lutgardita to fit him
for a uniform to wear to his death.

Y como fue otro José who went into exile
but returned with a box filled with poems
she stitched into the hems of her skirts and
scattered en los rincones de la casa de la Habana
where, años después, she prepares the parlor

to greet the ladies que vienen de visita
and pronounces: indiscutiblemente
César will have to grow accustomed to this

Lutgardita

takes in sewing to support herself
and Sisa, but refuses redondamente
to work for women. La fastidian
with their fastidious ways.

Men are menos exigentes.
She only needs to ask them
de qué lado lo cargan.

Clouds of Grief

In old age Aida could still see
the cloud of grief hovering
over her sister Quetica, lying still
in death on the same dining table
where Antonia had pushed her into life.

After the curb dealt the deadly blow
to Quetica's dark curls while she played
hopscotch outside la casa de Cienfuegos,
Aida's only comfort was that Miguelito
would no longer be alone, and Quetica
could surely embrace him without fear
of the measles, or tragic accidents,
or clouds of tears thundering below.

Papá del Loro

Joaquín walks through the door cradling
one of many creatures he would bring
home, decía Antonia, *de quién sabe dónde*—
a parrot sin plumas whom he names simply:
El Loro. Week after week he feeds the hatchling
by hand, sings softly to him, until feathers
blossom and throat opens to sound.

He teaches El Loro first to say *Antonia*,
then to repeat the names of his five children
and the names of each of las criadas. Finally
with a flourish he dubs himself: *Papá del Loro.*

El Loro flaps his wings wildly each night when
Papá returns from the distillery, dances happily
when Papá invites him to bailar la Chambelona,
serenades him con el Himno Nacional de Cuba,
perches on his left shoulder after dinner dishes
are cleared and the French doors to la terraza flung

open so that the family of yaguazas y la grulla Panchita
can gather close for the concerts Coro y Lula y Aida
y Quino play for him, the breeze carrying streams
of piano and strings and tenor tones into the darkness lit
by electric lamps and the harmonies orchestrated
by las manos de Papá

Despedida I

In the driveway de la casa de Cienfuegos
Aida approaches Ñico and asks in a low voice
if she can ride with him to la Habana when
he makes his monthly Chrysler delivery

and deliver her to their cousin's house for
a weekend visit. When they arrive Aida
kisses her prima on the cheek, unpacks
her maletín, and removes a letter she gives

to Ñico to deliver to their father, inviting Joaquín
to imagine he has sent his youngest daughter to
a boarding school for rich girls, rather than to work
for the cinco pesos a month she would send

home to pull the family out of the Depression
and the City of One Hundred Fires
smoldering in rivers of ash and ruin

Translating Aída

Ailalá Mena, ¿estás bien?
Esto, nieta, es para ti.
Cómprate los patos Í
y ve a casa de Carmén
Pipo te lleva con Ó
o te acompaña Cocó,
pero le dices a Ó
que no responda por ti.
Y despúes de tanta lata
se despide tu abuelito.
Recibe pues un besito
que te lo remite Tata.

José Basilio,
to his granddaughter Aída

José Basilio delights
   in his granddaughter's childish
      tongue tossing words
         into salads of syllables

and chides Abuelo Joaquín
   for attempting to translate Aída
      to those who do not inhabit a world
         in which all things black share
            the name of la criada Isabel

He did not know then that he need not
   worry, that her little girl tongue would grow
      to sprout words complete, fiery and fierce
         sin pelos en la lengua this woman
            who needs no translation

Wedding Bell

Although she was the family medium,
the spirits never told Tía María
that her husband would abandon her after
their first-born son was delivered quietly
into this world, already swaddled in the next

or that forty years later César would
hunt him down, demanding the divorce
that would allow her to marry Enrique,
who found her en la casa de la Habana Vieja,
and refused to let her go.

La familia from as far as Cienfuegos
streamed into the courthouse to the sound
of César joyously ringing the bronze bell
Aida used to summon their daughters to dinner,
and to the sight of Tía María's radiant blush, and
the soft smile spreading over Enrique's face

Rescue Operations

The air en la casa del Biltmore is thick
with the song of los tomeguines,
except when tropical storms roll
through and leave
the backyard trees hushed
and heavy with rain.

When el diluvio subsides
Lula hurries downstairs and invites
Alicia out to search
for fallen nidos, instructing
her budding apprentice to listen
for the soft cries of los pichoncitos, scan
the foliage for flashes
of tiny yellow tail feathers, approach
slowly to scoop them
up in tender hands, and lay them
suavecito in shoeboxes lined
with the newspapers Lula collects
for her rescue operations.

Alicia delights in learning
to feed los pichoncitos three times a day
with toothpicks dipped in cornmeal.
At night Lula keeps the shoeboxes
by her bed, lulled to sleep
by satisfied chirping, until
los tomeguines grow
wings deep green and strong
enough to be released
from her perch en el patio
where she beckons Alicia to make
a nest of interlocked fingers
from which each pajarito flies
to rejoin the throng,
adding their notes
to birdsong rising

Feathers

After Joaquín dies of heart failure
en la casa de Almendares
El Loro plucks out his plumas
one by one, refuses to repeat
words, or emerge from his cage.

Lula patiently nurses him back to
feathers, but never again to say
Papá del Loro. Some losses are
unspeakable, the recollection
of presence too acute a reminder

of absence. What became of him
then, when the family fled in a flood
of tears and left him behind
con familia en Cienfuegos?
Was there someone to greet him

when he woke from antediluvian
dreams, and teach him new names,
or did his throat close to the billowing
smoke, feathers singed and
fallen to the ground?

Sueños

In Memoriam Enrique González Mántici

Tío Kiko sleeps by day,
rises at dusk. He stands
erect, arms suspended
for just a moment
before raising the baton.
His wild hair dances
to the rhythm of his hands
directing la Sinfónica
that plays behind the mirror
of the armoire door.

María Mántici was fond
of saying that Kiko
had not been fathered
by her wayward husband,
but was conceived
when Beethoven came
to her bed en un sueño.

I wonder whether Beethoven
visited his son en sueños
after he woke
one evening to find
that everyone,
even his mother,
had left him behind.
What symphony
did he conduct
in silence standing
before the armoire mirror
reflecting crepuscular light?

The Things She Carried

A small suitcase and the statue
of la Virgen that Alicia asked
her to bring from among
the artifacts César had hidden
for Mother Thomas, the one
that had enchanted her nieta
since she first saw it sitting
on the bookshelf of her
second-grade classroom.

Traveling alone Antonia
surrenders to the stripping
of her clothes and the probing
hands of la miliciana by closing
her eyes and picturing Quetica
and Miguelito, remembering
that in eighty years she had
suffered trials more terrible.

Only when she fastens
the last button of her blusa
and la miliciana instructs
her to forfeit la Virgen and
her wedding ring does she
rebel and tell the woman
she will have to kill her first.

La miliciana raises her bayonet
in response, pierces the round
base of the statue, and thrusts
her hand inside in search
of hidden treasure. Finding no more
than she had found in the furrows
of Antonia's crevices, she returns
the hollow Virgen, abandons
the wedding ring, and allows
la cabrona anciana to board the plane.

As Antonia settles into her seat
a stewardess approaches, asks
whether she is willing to carry
a three-month-old baby flying
alone on the same exodus.
She places la Virgen gently
on the floor between her feet,
receives the whimpering
girl-child into her arms
and weeps.

Excavation

De niña Alicia sneaks into her father's study and slides
into her secret hiding place, the space
under the massive desk where César stretches
his legs, where she looks through the books
her mother has forbidden her to touch:

el libro de poesía de José Basilio—a thick ledger bound
in gray linen where her abuelo wrote his verses
and copied favorite poems in meticulous Gothic script

and her father's anatomy textbook, made
with brilliantly illustrated overlays
of each human system that Alicia peels back
in slow succession—skin, muscles and tendons,
arteries and veins and vital organs—until
she excavates the skeleton, runs her little girl finger
over each vertebra, each bone

and *La Hora 25* by Gheorghiu—perusing the pages
she cannot understand why the farmhand Moritz was sent
to the labor camp, but likes to pronounce
the author's name and ponder how there could be
more than twenty-four hours in a day.

De mujer Alicia gingerly touches the spine
of *La Hora 25* that now rests on her bookshelf, wary
of damaging its disintegrating cover, and wonders
why, of all the things he could have chosen, her father
carried this novel with him into exile

wishes she could go back and dig
up the books and bones that stayed behind

Mangrove Roots

Now I am a woman longing to be a tree, planted in a moist, dark earth/ Between sunrise and sunset—
Joy Harjo

Labyrinths

He naufragado en un universo de palabras,
pero sólo la palabra salva
arma única que he aprendido a empuñar
contra la soledad.
Lourdes Casal

You arrive, an annunciation at dawn,
when the aroma of café con leche,
the same color as your skin, consoles me

while I linger, longing for you to stay
por un ratico no más,
as when you crossed Mami's threshold
into our desperate arms

      (Elegguá saluted you
      ceded passage, beguiled
      by your laughter and song)

But you vanish, leaving me to wander
in the labyrinth of your words,
the only weapons you were able
to wield contra la soledad

      (Changó graced you
      with his fire, enamored
      by your word-flames)

and my memories
conjured from the soft folds
of your buoyant arms
holding me and Rafi
banishing my child grief

      por un ratico no más

Havana 1974

Although I have seen the faded photographs stuck
in album pages overlaid by peel-away plastic,
I do not remember standing on the crumbling
sea wall with Yoyo, Ricky, and Rafi at Guanabo,
a yellow salvavidas sitting on my six-year-old hip

> or staring at fireworks flowering in the night sky
> at el Carnaval de la Habana while Abuela Rosina held
> my hand, her long index finger directing my wide eyes
> to the massive papier-mâché heads bobbing along El Malecón.

There are no photographs of the coriaceous creases
on Abuelo César's face turn to stone, smooth and cold,
when Mami told him she had decided to take us back
to the island they had fled, on a mission to meet Papi's
parents, who had chosen to stay and stand with Fidel

> or of the raised rifle of the Mexico Embassy guard
> shooting the tire of the taxi as it pulled away when
> Mami set her first foot on the sidewalk, our bright Buster
> Browns still dangling from the sticky leather back seat

or of Mami's left leg shaking across from el agente
de Seguridad del Estado, a thick binder of unknown
contents before her and a portrait of el Che behind her,
answering the same questions for eight hours while we
played en el apartamento del Vedado con la gata Cecilia

> or of Mami's alabaster skin turn ash when Abuela Rosina
> reported that there were no re-entry papers to enable
> our return through México, *pero no te preocupes, hija,*
> *Ricardo lo resuelve con el consul Mexicano,* who was out
> of the country, but would surely respond to his call

or of the length of Mami's onyx hair laid on Papi's linen pillow,
her eyes scanning the room that remained as he left it lined
wall-to-wall with model World War II airplanes and the books

he amassed on his weekly visits to La Moderna Poesía, as she
wondered why he led her there, and how she might get us out

     or of the thick eyebrows of the Aeroflot ticket agent, raised
     over inscrutable eyes when Mami asked to buy three one-way
     tickets to Barbados, even if it meant she must spend all of her cash
     and leave her passport for approval hasta después del almuerzo

or of Mami's sandaled feet frozen on Calle la Rampa when
she heard the rapid footfall of the ticket agent running after her
begging in words hushed and hurried to deliver a message
to her sister María in Miami, that their father was dying and could
she please tell her how she had found the way to come home?

     or of months later María running down her gravel driveway,
     arms waving as Mami circled the block looking for the house
     on Southwest 6th Street, heralding that la Virgen de las Mercedes
     was hovering over our car accompanied by un alma poderoso
     with eyes green like mine and a dark mole on his left cheek.

I remember nothing. I only hear the sound of my mother drawing
words from wells deeper than grief, recounting our journey there
and back, on a mission she cannot comprehend, but believes was willed
by my father and Our Lady of Mercy, who hover over us still.

Ophelia Dying

After Papi died
Tía Tere and Tío Ricardo
took us in on weekends,
filled our slow, hot days
with backyard games and
my head with words and rhyme.

Tía Tere sang to me,
called me Rosa Mariposa,
made me feel I might
emerge from my chrysalis
and, maybe, someday

fly. I cried in darkness
when they flew,
weaving one more thread
into a tapestry of losses,
and you landed in their place.

You said your favorite word was
mariposa
swallowed my sprouting wings
syllable by syllable
ma-ri-po-sa
and smacked your lips
with each letter you claimed.

Abuela Makes Natilla

Rafi, Luis and I after school scurry
into la casa de la Doce Avenida,
through the gate framed
by flowering allamanda,
across el patio,
through sliding glass doors,
into the Florida room,
over the linoleum tiles
of Abuela Aida's kitchen,
and straight to la nevera

where we find
the orderly results
of her explosive culinary efforts:
neat rows of ramekins filled
with creamy yellow natilla con canela.

The ingredients are simple:
eggs, milk, sugar.
The trick, she would later teach me,
is to keep stirring

which I do now, and remember
the stores of sweetness
she gave us
to guard against bitterness

small acts writ large
sprinkled like cinnamon
to bless us on our way

Palabras for Coco

There are days when I wake
awash in your exuberant love

springing from the pores of your pale skin
peppered with the freckles you once
tried to remove with sewing pins,

chasing an ephemeral vision of beauty
with your characteristic folly,
longing for the wingéd love that landed

briefly, with brilliant plumes,
then flew, leaving you inocente
and hollow with yearning.

I wonder if you cried in the night for *¡Socorro!*
lamenting the bitter irony of your name
or if you eased into your role as favorite

tía unleashing oceanic love
upon the fruits of your sister's womb,
each of your desiccated ovum resurrected as

Palabra, pulsating
in the tents you erected for us
with bed sheets borrowed from Abuela Aida

en la casa de la Doce Avenida
where you beckoned us to enter, and listen
to word threads unraveling

until we opened our child eyes
in the City of One Hundred Fires agape
at the sight of Abuelo Joaquín's monkeys

waking you and your sibling brood,
nipping at bare toes peeking
from layers of mosquito net and linen.

These, your children,
leaping and swinging into eternity

Diagramming Sentences

Sitting upright at her desk, Mrs. Grinnell teaches us
to diagram sentences. Knitting needles dance on her lap

as she knits a blanket for her baby grandson. Lifting
her eyes over thin-rimmed reading glasses, she points

one of her needles at me, signaling my turn to approach
the chalkboard and dissect the next sentence.

I love diagramming sentences. Identifying the subject
and predicate of the independent clause, so named,

Mrs. Grinnell explains, because it can stand alone
as a complete thought. Writing each one neatly on

a straight horizontal axis, then dividing them
with a short vertical line. Placing the subordinate clause

on the diagonal beneath the horizontal line, incorporating
the fragile dependence of an incomplete thought.

After school I unpack my books en la mesa de la cocina
while Abuela brings me my merienda, which I eat

slowly so that I can listen closely and decipher
whether the same rules of grammar apply to Spanish

as to English. Abuela strings together sentences that tell
of her life in Cuba, of all that she left behind.

La casa del Biltmore. Tía María. The flowers Tío Quino
planted en el jardín. El Loro de Papá. Her father's bones.

And of all that she and Abuelo had planted en el exilio.
Her nietos playing Parchese in the Florida room

de la casa de la Doce. Gardenias in glasses on
the kitchen sill. Natilla con canela en la nevera.

Closing my eyes, I diagram her sentences
on the backs of my eyelids and watch with wonder as

I see the constructions take shape. That loss
is always written on the diagonal, always
subordinate to grace.

Poem In Which I Find My Mother

who I never really lost, except
for a time when I was twelve
and began to roll my eyes
at her eyes forever looking back
to the island she left behind.

Annoyed by her spinning
the same stories
of how the blue sky was bluer
and the fine sand was finer,
I mocked her once in public,
in the musty auditorium at
Saints Peter and Paul

until I looked up and saw
her laughing features fall
and grow dark
as she stood up
and walked out proudly through
the heavy double doors.

Those island stories I now roll
silkily on my tongue,
like the butterscotch candies
wrapped in gold that she would press
into my hand when I was sad
and no one was looking

and wish I could taste again
when my daughters roll their eyes
at my eyes always looking back
to days of butterscotch sweetness
where I find my mother spinning
and weaving her story strands
into my own

Love Language

I was twenty-three years old when I learned
my abuelo's language

spoken in syllables round
like the avocados bright
green and smooth
he shook furiously from
his backyard tree
and deposited by the dozens
into cardboard boxes
he shipped from Miami to Georgia
after I lamented the state
of aguacates small
and shriveled like raisins
at my corner grocery store

and formed into sentences certain and straight
like the six-hundred and sixty-four miles of Interstate
he drove to bring me shriveled home

Last Words

I search my memory
for Abuelo César's last words
but can only remember
his face, yellow
and pinched with pain,
slowly giving way to ease

and am grateful to Abuela
for following me out
of his room, speaking for him:

Hija, tú lo hiciste tan feliz

Despedida II

After she falls and breaks
her hip, Abuela slips
slowly into the abyss.

The hand that always held
her compass so firmly now
shoots up, translucent
and trembling, in desperate
beckoning to the sisters
and brothers who call to her
from the dim hallways
de la casa de Cienfuegos.

She cries out to them,
calls them by name—
¡Coro! ¡Lula! ¡Ñico!
¡Quino! ¡Quetica! ¡Miguelito!—
but cannot find her way
to the voices that echo
in the crumbling labyrinth
of fragmented memory.

Our grief is tempered
with relief when the dark
corners are illuminated and
voice and hand together
fall silent.

In the ensuing stillness,
her daughters gently
bathe her body,
brush her hair,
anoint her with perfume
and cover her limbs lovely
with the rose-colored quilt
folded at the foot of her bed,
a prayer tied into each knot
to keep her warm

while I bow my head
to Abuela's hand raised
firm and steady
en bendición.

Triduum

I.   Holy Thursday

In the half light of dawn
we drive up the road
edged with royal palms
to the entrance of Baptist Hospital.

Mami has come to be broken open
understanding, finally, that
she must be broken open
to rise and walk again.

I shudder to leave her, shivering
laid out on cold, metal slab
bathed in iodine prelude to the scalpel
poised in the surgeon's delicate hand.

One hour passes.
The surgeon emerges, says
all is well, promising
she will walk—even dance!—again.

II.   Good Friday

Her room is shrouded in darkness
punctuated by the steady hum
of machines and anxious whispers.
She cannot rise as expected,

body not responding to will.
The color drains from her face
throwing her small moles into relief.
The nurse calls for fresh blood

while I hold vigil
praying to the dead
my litany for the living

Papi, pray for us
Abuelo y Abuela, pray for us
Coco y Nana, pray for us

III.   Holy Saturday

I seek respite en la casa de Mentone Street
but I cannot sleep, overwhelmed by the scent
of lavender and Listoline, and candles
lit for the intentions of her children.

The wood plank floors warp as
our ghosts pass through their cracks,
breaking through the glass-encased tombs
arranged in patterns on the walls,

pulling chairs around the domino table,
passing cafecitos laced with laughter,
the clic clac of ivory tiles setting
a new rhythm.

Laying in her bed
I conjure them all, trusting
they will roll away her stone
take her pale hands into theirs
and lead her out
to dance and sing again

¿Y Tu Abuela Dónde Está?

Aquí el que no tenga dinga
Tiene mandinga…¡ja, ja!
Por eso te pregunto
¿Y tu agüela, aonde ejtá?
Fortunato Vizcarrondo

When Abuelo Rafael finally flees
  Cuba and lands en la casa de University Drive
  my tongue is burning with questions

like what is the origin of our strange last name?
  Intentó, he tells me, to dredge the roots
  of our family tree, until he arrived

en Trinidad where, he whispers,
  uno era o negro o negrero.
  So he traced his steps back

to la Habana, wanting, he says,
  sitting up straight in his chair,
  to know no more.

Love Letters, 1960-63

On my mother's bedroom shelf
I find the crimson leather
volume binding love

letters mailed across ninety miles,
delivered sixty years later
to daughter hands

afraid to unfold them. Afraid
to drown in oceans of salt
tears. Afraid of chest heave

gasping for air. Marveling
that words can form such waves
of grief, and love, and loss.

Shark Swimming

They call him the Shark Man,
says the reporter, introducing
a diver who swims
with great whites so close
he can see the color
of their eyes, grab a dorsal fin
and go for a ride. The Shark Man
advises the television audience that,
above all, you must remain perfectly
calm when swimming with sharks.

Mami learned this from Papi
the day she dove
into Havana Harbor
from the sailboat they rented
for the day. She did not know then
that the waters were teeming
with sharks scavenging
for scraps tossed by sailors
from incoming ships,
until her eyes met the spread
wide eyes of a hammerhead
and she thrashed
her way back up to the boat.
Papi pulled her in and held her close
until she could breathe again
explaining gently that,
were she ever to encounter
another shark, she must be
still and glide
slowly to the surface.

I have not yet mastered this move
to not move
in panic when swimming with sharks.
Like my mother I
rise terrorized

through the choppy sea
land in rocking boats
a beached fish
flapping
fins bleached
in the unforgiving sun

Cachita At My Throat

I remember only at the long end
of the day.

You would have cumplido
seventy. For forty-two years
no mañanitas inviting you to rise
and greet the dawn. No birthday
cakes from Edda's Bakery.
We have not seen you grow old.

Yo no cumplí.
Lost on a quest
for flip flops to wear
on a beach vacation,
I forgot you.

But you remembered me,
guiding my hand
to your mother's medalla,
shades of faded
gold and lapis at my throat,
congealing into image:
La Virgen de la Caridad,
hovering over los tres Juanes
who would have surely drowned without her.

She did not intercede for you,
though you strung her around your neck
across ninety miles to foreign shore.
Mami unclasped the chain
from your stiffening throat,
held it in her cupped hands

to give me, who wear it now
Cachita at my throat.
I imagine your skin touching mine
through her intervention.

As I rub her gently between
thumb and forefinger
she plunges me into the tempest.
Falling overboard
I sink into water depths
swim through sunken wrecks
scrape my legs on barnacle growth.
Startled I stare into shark eyes,
glide through the water
green eyes open to salt
resurface

to see her, your emissary,
Cachita, Oshún
rising from the furious sea
pulling me up into the small boat
covering me with blue kisses.

We row to shore.

Relajo en El Carajo

Do I know you?
      I see the words dance on my computer screen, a siren call
      in cyberspace from a woman I do not know, yet who shares my name

Do I know you?
      so I set sail on blood currents in search of my father's roots
      to an impromptu Prohías family reunion (or meet and greet,
      as Rafi prefers to call a gathering of relatives we've never met)
      at El Carajo, a tapas bar tucked into the back of a gas station
      and LA Food Mart on the corner of 17th Avenue and Dixie Highway

Do I know you?
      I ask myself, scrutinizing the faces around the table
      as we pass croquetas and chorizo and copas de sangria,
      dismembering their features, looking for resemblances
      that might help me re-member and refashion my father
      with the flesh and bones of those who bear his name

Do I know you?
      I listen to Marta and Yoly tell of three brothers,
      descendants of Grecian sailors, who followed their current
      of ancestral restlessness from the port in Palamós
      to Trinidad where, it is whispered, the brothers were reft
      when one gave his hand in marriage to a black woman

Do I know you?
      Marta imagines the jubilant clan in heaven having
      their own reunion, an eternal party of ever-flowing
      Cuba Libres, where they decide to maneuver us
      like marionettes and bring our tributaries together,
      converging in a splendid sea of family en El Carajo,
      at the corner of 17th Avenue and Dixie Highway

      the unlikely lookout point where I stand
      and search for dry land
      and a place to plant
      myself

Primo

For Yoyo

Me da gracia
when you explain
words and phrases
to me, your gringa cousin,
as if fifty years and ninety miles
could dilute my mother's milk

as if *vieja*
(an affectionate term,
you say, referring to one's mother)
could taste any different
on my tongue than yours,
whether released with relish
into Miami or Havana
salt air.

And so I laugh
when you introduce
Carajo.

Definition:
An indiscrete term
signifying Hell,
or a faraway place.

Origin:
The lookout,
or highest point
on ancient ships,
where sailors were sent
as punishment
for their transgressions.

But after awhile
la gracia

no me da gracia.
The hand of grace
raised
in blessing over our heads
turns menacing,
the sugar on my tongue
drowns in bile

and rage
at the distance
that makes you think
you must translate at all.

Así es.
You stand perched
(parched)
in your carajo.
I stand in mine.
Each squinting
blindly
at a blank horizon

Cross Currents

Yoyo yearns to learn about all that is American,
listening to classic rock and, when his luck allows him
to secretly latch onto the WiFi at the Cohiba Hotel,
reading Wikipedia pages about Jefferson and Lincoln,
carefully preparing for replanting in the soil
that will send his branches sprawling upward.

My branches tend toward Cuban palms, rumba
and guaguancó, and the waves crashing on El Malecón
where I once stood holding Abuela Rosina's hand,
but cannot remember, longing to return,
as Yoyo said, *a la tierra que casi te engendró,*
to water my roots with currents of blood and belonging

On Our Second Night in Havana

For Tía Ivette

you tell us stories, feverishly.

The breeze from your balcón cannot bear
the weight of cigarette smoke
and words that hang, heavy
like your desperation.

I choke on El Período Especial,
when the Soviet ships pulled out
taking the food with them

when clouds of smoke could not overpower
the stench of the horse strapped by its hooves
blood draining before slashing for meat
to carry home in hiding to your children

or mask the gratitude on your bloodless face.

In the Absence of Paper

On our last day in Havana
Yoyo takes me and Mami to
La Feria, where I set off
alone in search of a figure
of la Virgen de la Caridad
and the note paper I did not
think to bring in my gusano
bag stuffed with baby clothes,
bottles, and diapers for Olivia,
shampoo and soap for Ivette.

Finding neither, I find Yoyo
sitting on a bench by the harbor
and ask, *¿Dónde puedo encontrar papel,*
to write your mother a note before I go?
He laughs, repeats the now familiar
refrain—*No es fácil*—adding,
En Cuba no hay papel
ni pá los médicos escribir recetas.

But in the absence of paper
where will I leave her my heart
to unfold and hold close in the night?

Lasciate Ogni Revisited

Nunca se regresa a Ítaca.
Las razones son obvias.
Lourdes Casal

Adrift in the tempest
you dreamed with Odysseus
returning to Ithaca
bare toes sinking into sand
Argus waiting to greet you on the shore.

In West Side waking
you discovered there is no return
(Heraclitus and his river,
entre otras cosas)
least of all in memory.

Today I dream with you.
We walk
leaving weary Odysseus behind.
I invite Penelope instead
to help us weave words
luminous in the waning light.

The Canopy

we need the flutter that can save us,
something that will swirl across the face
of what we have become and bring us grace.
Lucille Clifton

Las verdades elementales caben en el ala de un colibrí.
José Martí

Prayer for Grace

Mine, O thou lord of life, send my roots rain.
Gerard Manley Hopkins

Sometimes grace comes not
swift and sudden in the burning bush

but dripping slow, seeping
into parched soil

each drop an offering
of fragile hope that the roots

may hold
and grow to fullness

Inheritance

Abuela Aida was obsessed with whether
her daughters would sprout las orejas de torreja
de Abuelo César y José Basilio, those ears
that induced Sisa to tie a blue ribbon around
Tío Raul's infant head (even if people might think
he was a girl) to prevent them from smothering
him in his sleep. She gave thanks to God when
Mami and Mina each emerged from the womb
with ears well-proportioned for wearing a proper
moño, and again years later, when we her nietos
also managed to escape the elephantine curse.
So when our first daughter is born the women
of the family ceremoniously swoop down to dissect
her baby body. Mami proclaims que la niña tiene
las sortijitas pegadas a la cabeza like my father,
though the strawberry blond hue of her ringlets
belongs to Abuela Rosina. Most importantly, her ears
are perfect, tiny caracoles de nacar. Lying in her moisés,
la niña gazes at her father, not yet able to recognize
the amused smile taking shape as he strokes the reddish
stubble of his beard, while I fix my eyes on hers, wanting
to believe it's true, that a little piece of ourselves
can live in the precise curve of a fingernail bed,
or in the pupil of the bluest eye

The Color of Music

Be not afraid; the isle is full of noises,
Sounds and sweet airs that delight and hurt not.
William Shakespeare

The color of music is mauve
in my world, you assert,
as when you were a child younger than now

The word itself, that is,
purply plump and palpable
suspended in a space I cannot see

The notes, infinite in number,
are variegated in hue
each one a particular shade

and gift unveiling
the precise point
on your trombone slide

where you must stop and hold.
A flat arrives in a flood of gray
B sharp a burst of burnt orange

Black notes on a white page
illegible to me, your mother,
sing to you in kaleidoscopic joy

I listen, in wonder longing
to have my synapses fire red
like your name

to be so in tune
with the vibrations of the spheres
quivering

each word, each sound
always more than it seems
in a symphony of light

First Flown

On our first morning
the nurse brought you,
hungry and screaming,
to me, so nauseated
I refused to feed you

until she, unrelenting
turned my weary weight
left and lay
you, first born,
by my side
your oval mouth seeking
and finding my breast.

And so first loved
on first morning
you pushed me
to the edge of fear
and over

wondrous free fall
into waters
unfathomable
which we plumbed together
hands held fast
through your fears
of the clank of heater pipes
and claw of hermit crab

and mine, of easing my grip
on your freckled hand
to let you climb
to the edge
where you stand now

first flown
wingspan broad

breath
taking flight
as I watch, and feel
the surge in my breast heavy
still
with milk

Broken Things

Pouring water into the coffee maker, my hand
slips and knocks the mug to the floor. Time
slows as I watch it fall and hit the unforgiving tile—
the handle first to break off, then crack in half as
the rim shatters into jagged pieces at my feet.
My favorite mug, the first one I brought home
from The Dancing Turtle near the end of the road
on Hatteras Island. The first one I reach for blindly
every morning seeking comfort in the way it nestles
into my fingers curled around the North Carolina clay,
thrown by someone who loved it to life and purpose,
tinted in shades of mossy green and dusty rose, passing
love forward to my hands that cradle hope as I sip,
and inhale the scent of coffee and salty breezes blowing
in from the Atlantic, and my little girls' voices rising
above the music of lapping waves as they gather
shells, and their father rejoicing in the fresh catch
of marlin and wahoo he tosses on the hot grill, and
the flutter of plover wings escaping our greyhounds'
enthusiastic attempts to catch the little birds in flight.

The scent of a time before I learned
that love is as fragile as fired clay,
so easily broken into shards
scattered on the kitchen floor.

Dar a Luz

When Abuela Aida arrived at the edge
of despair, ready to let the child
wither inside her womb
after two days of fruitless labor

Antonia burst into the birthing
room, told her daughter to hold on
to the cloths she tied to the bed rails
and follow her lead, until Aida,
nearly broken, breathed and pushed
the eleven-pound baby into the light.

Today Antonia came into my room,
this time soft of foot, whispering
respira profundo, mi'ja,
and keep pushing, and trust
that new life will come
even if you think you will break

Breaking Open the Word

Compartir—to share

I slice it neatly
turning the parts,
prefix and root,
in the palms of my hands

Com—with; together
Partir—to break

I savor the sweetness
of revelation
in division
to share is to break with
together
This is my body, broken for you

I break it open
La parto
again
this time conjugating
the root

Parto
Verb—I break
Noun—childbirth

and I remember

my legs splayed
releasing
and receiving
the bloodied, glorious cry
This is my body, broken for you

Then, the recoupling
the final conjugal act:

Comparto

I break with
for you
and there is birth
in the breaking

of body
of bread
of the Word

In Defense of Wheelbarrows

after William Carlos Williams

So much depends
upon
convincing you

so much depends
upon
a red wheelbarrow

that its utilitarian
form
can be transformed

by a glaze of rain and
gathering
of white chickens

that its weathered depths
can hold
a promise
tender
in a wash of morning light

Etymologies

Bone-tired I dig
with raw fingers into
the red Virginia clay

to unearth the twisted roots
begging to be pulled

uncovering pain
which, I explain, as I bundle
them in your tender palms,
is the root of compassion.

I keep digging
releasing so many roots

wonder words woven
into poems I yearn to
translate, so they may carry
you on their gnarled backs

from where you stand
to the land of your belonging

God Heals

The Archangel Rafael arrives broken.

He who protected Tobias on his trek
alights from his journey with fractured
wing. His severed right arm, once extended
to heaven, reveals a grisly stump. His left
hand lies forlorn in layers of bubble wrap,
reaching impotently for the gilded fish
that lies just beyond his grasp.

I despair. In such a state he will not
be able to stir stagnant pools, or lift
the murky mist from blinded eyes.

So I carefully wrap wing, arm, and hand in folds
of newsprint and deliver my broken angel
to the Chinese healer, whose only religion is Beauty.
Wordlessly he turns the lonely limbs in weathered
hands, examines them with bright eyes that look up
to meet mine, assuring me he can mend what is rent.

I return on Tuesday. The old man emerges
serenely from the back room and lays San Rafael
in my expectant arms. I take him home, place him
gently on the turned wood column in the corner
next to my chair, where he stands, poised for flight,
gilded fish in hand, arm outstretched to heaven

heralding his name:
God heals.

Word Blossoms

My daughter chafes at checking
boxes, as if identity could be bound
by lines on a pre-printed form.
Her seventh-grade self is faced
with the false choice of "Hispanic"
or "White." Sighing, she chooses
the latter, saying she doesn't really
feel Hispanic, or even speak much Spanish.

I wilt at that moment, one of many when
we discover that our children live beyond
the plots we prepare for them.

Now grown, she tells me there are words
that come to her only in Spanish:
moco, mantilla, cariñito.
I smile at the odd assortment, and revel
in the gentle rustle of leaves
on branches of trees
planted long ago.

When My First Daughter Tells Me

that she is content
to sip a cup of coffee
slowly in bed as morning
light streams through her
bedroom window, and gaze
at the row of three hot pink potted
succulents sitting
on the jewel green sill

I see
that the time has come
for reversals—

for her to teach and
release me

My Second Daughter Writes a Poem

about a dress
I gave her this

morning saying
it no longer fit

me, but would
look likely lovely

on her. I am
lost in self

excoriation for
allowing again

my body to grow
fat with regret

for who I am
not

when she dons
the dress revels

in fabric skimming
hips swaying

as she walks
on cobblestones

writes a poem
transforming herself

refashioning me.

Ring of Light

My mother was fifteen years old when
   she first admired it on Abuela Luz's elegant hand

en el apartamento del Vedado. She was twenty-nine
   when Rosina fulfilled her mother's wish and slipped it

onto Mami's widowed finger, the onyx oval nestled
   in an intricate bed of gold crafted by Abuelo Jorge

from the melted wedding rings of their parents,
   the molten melding of families rising above fire

Colando Café

It is 4:00pm
and Mami prepares
the afternoon ritual.

She reaches for the cuchara
that has taken up residence in
the red and yellow Bustelo can,
and scoops the warm, dark grounds.

She grasps the rubber-tipped cucharita
living with its kin in
the top drawer de la cocina

(utensils, like people, need a home
todo tiene su lugar)

and packs the granules
tightly
into the upper chamber of la cafetera.

She turns on the flame.

Standing sentinel
she awaits the alchemy
scrutinizing
lest the liquid overflow the spout,
or explode.

Sliding hot metal to cool coil
she pours,
evenly,
into mismatched cups
and passes each one,
a poem,
to eager hands that receive the gift
with gracias
Grace.

Acknowledgments

Thank you to the editors of the publications in which the following poems first appeared:

The Acentos Review: "The Color of Music"

Mas Tequila Review: "Breaking Open the Word"

Pilgrimage Magazine: "Primo"

Blue Lyra Review: "Colando Café"

Saw Palm: Florida Literature and Art: "On Our Second Night in Havana," "Lasciate Ogni Revisited"

Temenos Journal: "Prayer for Grace"

Postcard Poems and Prose: "Dar a Luz"

No Tender Fences: An Anthology of Immigrant and First-Generation American Poetry: "Raíces," "¿Y Tu Abuela Dónde Está?"

SWWIM Every Day: "Inheritance"

Sin Fronteras/Writers Without Borders: "Word Blossoms"

Gyroscope Review: "Triduum," "Broken Things"

And heartfelt thanks...

to Richard Blanco, Li Yun Alvarado, and Dawn Leas for so generously reading and responding to my manuscript;

to the extraordinary women in my writing group—Elisabeth Auld, Kathy Callahan, Paige Conner Totaro, Susan Fleischman, and Vero Autphenne—for giving me the friendship, feedback, and deadlines that allowed me to complete this project;

to my brothers Rafi and Luis, fellow mangrove dwellers, for plucking me from the waters of self-doubt;

to our mother Alicia, for sheltering us in her ceiba skirts and sharing the ancestral stories that shaped us;

to my daughters Ana and Sofia, mis pajaritos, for inspiring this collection;

and to my husband Bob, for his unconditional love, constant encouragement, and inexhaustible patience. "We die and rise the same and prove/ Mysterious by this love."

BIO

Rosie Prohías Driscoll is a Cuban-American educator and poet. The daughter and granddaughter of Cuban exiles, she writes about themes of identity and exile, loss and renewal, grief and grace. Her poems have appeared in numerous publications, including *Acentos Review, Mas Tequila Review, Literary Mama, Saw Palm: Florida Literature and Art, SWWIM Every Day, Sin Fronteras/Writers Without Borders, Pensive: A Global Journal of Spirituality and the Arts,* and *Gyroscope Review,* and she was a finalist for the 2020 Orison Poetry Prize. Raised in Miami, Florida, she received a bachelor's degree in English from Georgetown University and a master's degree in English and Comparative Literature from Emory University. She teaches high school English in Alexandria, Virginia, where she lives with her husband, their greyhound, and a host of ancestral spirits who keep her rooted and grateful. When not teaching or writing, she relishes spending time with friends and family and researching her family tree. *Poised for Flight* is her first full-length poetry collection.